Original title:
Snow Joke, It's Cold!

Copyright © 2024 Creative Arts Management OÜ
All rights reserved.

Author: Harris Montgomery
ISBN HARDBACK: 978-9916-94-266-6
ISBN PAPERBACK: 978-9916-94-267-3

Chilling Puns on the Frost

When the winter comes, oh what a sight,
Icicles dangling, shivering tight.
I asked the freeze if it was a friend,
It just chuckled, 'This is how I blend!'

The snowflakes dance, with a giggle and twirl,
I slipped on ice, gave my pride a whirl.
'Why did the chill blush?' I asked with a grin,
'It saw the warm sun and couldn't hold in!'

The Comedy of Cold Breezes

A frosty breeze whispered a pun,
'I'm just here to chill, let's have some fun!'
I donned my gloves, a hat on my head,
But my frozen toes felt like lead.

The snowmen chuckle as we pass them by,
With carrot noses and a frosty eye.
'Why don't they play hide and seek?' I jest,
'Because they always get caught in the frostiest quest!'

Frigid Follies Unfurled

As the cold weather rolled into town,
I wore my smile, despite the frown.
'Got any heat?' I shouted to the moon,
It laughed, 'I can't, I'll melt like a cartoon!'

With every snowball, laughter would flare,
'What do you call a flake with flair?'
'A star that just wanted a bit of light,
But fell for winter, oh what a fright!'

Hilarity in a Frozen Landscape

In a world of frost, the fun can ignite,
With jokes so chilly, they're out of sight.
Why did the snowman get a degree?
It was snow smart, as funny could be!

The winter wind howls a cheeky tune,
Suggesting everyone dance with a dune.
I asked if it snowed on the moon so far,
It replied, 'Only when it's party rad!'

Icy Reflection

The mirror shows a frozen face,
With icicles as my new embrace.
My breath dances in the air,
While neighbors blink in shock and stare.

I slip on socks, two lefts in play,
My coffee's chilled, what a fine day!
I built a snowman in my yard,
He's got my hat, it's rather hard.

I laughed so loud, it turned to ice,
My winter wit? Not so precise.
I ponder if I can still sing,
With frozen lips, a funny thing!

So I embrace this frosty plight,
Where every breath brings pure delight.
Chillin' out, I hope for sun,
'Till then, let's freeze and have some fun!

Frostbitten Lullaby

At night the stars just twinkle bright,
But all my toes have taken flight.
They're frozen solid, snug and still,
While penguins dance upon the hill.

I sip hot cocoa, marshmallows drown,
Yet still feel like the talk of town.
My cheeks are red, like cherry pie,
Why did I walk outside? Oh my!

The wind's a joker, pulls my hat,
With every gust, I squeak and chat.
The world is white, a fluffy mess,
My sense of balance? I confess.

In dreams I'm sliding as a pro,
While laughing as I tumble, whoa!
Oh winter nights, with icy cheer,
You make me smile, though cold is near!

Cold Comfort

Wrapped in layers, like a burrito,
Each move I make feels like a feat, oh!
The thermostat is on the blink,
It surely must be on the brink.

I've lost my gloves, a dreadful fate,
My fingers freeze, they contemplate.
Yet here I sit, a couch potato,
Wishing I could dance like Plato.

The kettle's boiling, whistling loud,
While neighbors sway, all snug and proud.
I put on socks that don't quite match,
A fashion statement, what a catch!

So let the frost and chill abound,
I'll stay inside, safe and sound.
With laughs and warmth around the fire,
Let's brew some tea, and never tire!

Winter's Muse

A snowflake lands upon my nose,
I giggle as my laughter grows.
The world is decked in sparkling cheer,
With frozen moments, crystal clear.

Outside I see a comical scene,
A dog in boots, so bright and keen.
He tries to chase a fluffy ball,
But tumbling down? He's sure to fall!

With red-nosed friends, we roam the lanes,
Our cheeks aglow, like heatless flames.
We throw some snow, a friendly fight,
With laughter ringing through the night.

As snowmen gather, hats a-fly,
We dance and sing beneath the sky.
In winter's chill, we find a muse,
In every flake, a life to choose!

Biting Frost

Frigid air nips at my nose,
My fingers feel like frozen toes.
Every step is quite a feat,
Like walking on a slippery sheet.

Penguins laugh as they slide by,
Wearing tiny hats, oh my!
While my cheeks turn bright like roses,
I'm just waiting for warm doses.

My breath puffs out like a cloud,
Each giggle echoes, oh so loud!
The icicles hang, a glistening sight,
As I frolic, feeling light.

Why did the snowman call in sick?
He found the chill just too much of a trick!
Time to bounce into the light,
Where warmth comes in, just out of sight.

Laughter in a Snowdrift

Covered in layers, I waddle with glee,
As my friends toss snowballs, aiming for me.
With each quick turn, I stumble and fall,
And the snow plops down, a soft white ball.

Why did the bird stay inside today?
It heard it was too cold to play!
But the flakes keep dancing, gliding and twirling,
While snowflakes in hats keep playfully swirling.

When I slip and land on my bum,
The laughter erupts—it's so much fun!
Like silly kids in a winter embrace,
We roll in the snow, lost in the race.

With frosty cheeks and hearts full of cheer,
We shout winter's verses, joyful and clear.
In this chilly realm, where spirits are high,
We'll dance with the frost, under a grey sky.

Frigid Fables

Once a snowman thought he'd try,
To surf on ice—it didn't fly!
He slipped and slid across the ground,
While giggles echoed all around.

A penguin joked, "You'll freeze your brains!"
While the snowflakes fell like little chains.
The frost had fun, playing its pranks,
As everyone joined in the laughs and shanks.

A bear in boots roamed with flair,
Bursting with laughter, beyond compare.
"I'm ready for winter," he shouted with glee,
"Still, I'd love a hot cocoa, just for me!"

At night, the stars, they twinkle so bright,
The cold can't freeze this sheer delight.
So remember this tale of laughter and cheer,
Winter's a playground we hold so dear.

Frosty Haikus

Chilblains and snowballs,
Laughter echoes through the cold,
Slipping, sliding fun.

Winter's icy breath,
Wraps us tight in giggles warm,
Boots squeak on the ground.

Snowflakes fall like dreams,
Bundled up, we dance with joy,
Frost nips, but we grin.

In a blanket of white,
Frolicking with frosty friends,
Memories like flakes.

Cold-Hearted Humor

The frostbitten man lost his shoes,
Now he walks around in a pair of blues.
Tried to warm up with a steaming tea,
But it turned into a frozen sea.

His fingers are numb, his nose is red,
He made a snowman with a ball for a head.
It winked at him, with a carrot smile,
Then collapsed, melting in a little while.

The Winter Giggle

Once I slipped on a patch of ice,
Fell down laughing, oh, isn't that nice?
The snowflakes danced as I took a dive,
Making frosty angels, feeling alive.

My hat flew off, it soared so high,
I waved goodbye as it touched the sky.
A pine cone landed right on my nose,
Laughter erupts as the chilly wind blows.

Icy Import

A penguin sneaks into my warm home,
Slides on the floor like he's here to roam.
He spills my cocoa with a flippered sway,
And laughs like he just got paid today.

His frosty breath brings a gust of fun,
While I try to catch him, but I've just begun.
He waddles away, with my doughnut in hand,
Leaving me chuckling, oh isn't it grand!

Frigid Farce

A snowball fight turned into a game,
Where even the dog tried to stake his claim.
He wagged his tail and jumped in delight,
Then plopped in a pile, looking quite white.

I aimed for my friend and missed by a mile,
The cold hit my back, but I had to smile.
With laughter echoing through the white ground,
Who knew winter could be so profound?

Giggles in the Glaciers

In the land where frostbits play,
Snowmen dance the night away.
With carrot noses, they jive,
Who knew ice could come alive?

Penguins waddle, doing tricks,
Sipping cocoa, sharing quips.
Polar bears in fuzzy hats,
What a sight - they look like cats!

Flakes like feathers dance in glee,
Frosty air, a comedy.
Snowball fights in silly rounds,
Laughter echoes, joy abounds.

Chill the air, but hearts are warm,
In this jest, we'll find our charm.
With each slip and frosty fall,
We burst out laughing, one and all.

Frosty Folly

Icicles hang like fangs of glee,
Mittens lost, where could they be?
Sleds like rockets, speeding fast,
In the snow, we giggle past.

Jack Frost's painted on each pane,
With every chill, we feel the gain.
Snowflakes whisper, soft and light,
Tickling noses, what a sight!

Skating on ponds like we're bold,
Falling down, but never sold.
With frosty breath, we make a cheer,
This winter wonderland's so dear.

Hot chocolate spills, oh what a mess,
Who can resist this winter dress?
In frozen moments, funny and bright,
Together we laugh, into the night.

Laughter Amidst the Chill

Hats askew, we bundle tight,
Chasing flakes in pure delight.
Each chilly breeze brings giggles new,
Watch out for that snowball, too!

Ski poles waving, laughter shared,
Falling hard, no one is spared.
Snow forts built like castles grand,
Pretend kings with icy sand.

Frozen fingers, noses red,
Comedic slips, and giggles spread.
With every tumble, joy we find,
In this frosty world, we unwind.

As night falls on this icy stage,
Tickling winds, we laugh with rage.
Winter's filled with merry scenes,
A blanket of joy, bright and keen.

Winter's Hidden Puns

Under layers of frosty haze,
Laughter melts the coldest days.
Puns on tongues, tongues in cheeks,
Winter humor, what fun it seeks!

Slippery sidewalks, watch your step,
Hold your breath, and try your rep.
Giggles erupt at each misstep,
Falling snowflakes, never inept.

Chili days with giggling friends,
In the whirlwind, laughter blends.
With snowballs thrown and faces bright,
Winter's humor shines so right.

Tripping on snow, we take a bow,
Proclaiming victory, here and now.
Amidst the chill, we find our fun,
In the winter sun, we're all as one.

Comical Cold Snap

Winter's chill has come to play,
Laughing winds in disarray.
Mittens lost, a scarf unspun,
Fingers frozen, oh what fun!

Parks are white, a frosty maze,
Snowmen grinning, in a daze.
Kids all slip like silly fish,
Landing flat, it's quite the dish!

Cars are stuck in icy grips,
Drivers curse and crack their lips.
Hot cocoa spills on wooly hats,
Cheers abound in frosty spats!

Bundle tight, the world's a laugh,
Sleds and laughter on the path.
With all the slips, it's hard to frown,
In this winter wonder clown!

Frosted Ironies

The sun peeks through a frosty haze,
As icicles hang in gleeful ways.
A warm cup spills as lovers flee,
In chase of warmth, it's quite the spree!

Cats in coats look quite absurd,
Dashing fast, their tails a blur.
Crisp leaves crunch like popcorn made,
In the icy dance that winter laid.

Frosty breath and rosy cheeks,
Everybody falls; laughter peaks.
Timid slips turn bold and bright,
Gather 'round for a snowball fight!

Penguin waddles down the street,
Silly strut upon his feet.
In this chill, we find our grace,
Against the laughter, we embrace!

Slippery Smiles

Underfoot, a slick surprise,
Tumbling toddlers, gleeful cries.
With helmets on and snowballs in tow,
Each fall becomes a comedy show!

Ice skating feats turn into slips,
Arms flailing, oh how he flips!
Mom's warm cookies, a tantalizing scent,
But she just laughs, "That was not meant!"

A dog in boots walks like a king,
Chasing snowflakes, what joy they bring.
Teary eyes from laughter's blast,
These moments make the winter last.

With each fall, we'll giggle and cheer,
For winter's fun is finally here!
Through frosted laughs, we find our way,
In slippery smiles, we'll dance and play!

Brilliantly Blustery

Gusty winds that swirl and twirl,
Balloons take flight in a messy whirl.
Hats take off, a wild race,
Chasing them brings smiles to face!

Sleds collide in a joyful heap,
Laughter rings, not a single peep.
Footprints wander, zig and zag,
As frosty air makes laughter brag!

Bundle up, yet somehow freeze,
Hot laughter floats in the brisk breeze.
Every drip from dripping nose,
Turns to giggles, and oh, who knows?

Brilliantly blustery, here it pours,
Winter's charm, all fun outdoors.
Through chilly air and joyful prance,
We'll embrace this snowy dance!

Frosted Dreams

Beneath the fluff, the world is white,
Fingers freeze with sheer delight.
A snowman grins with carrot nose,
While chill seeps in from toes to clothes.

Children giggle, throw some flakes,
What's that sound? A snowball breaks!
Slip and slide on icy sheen,
Winter's canvas, oh so clean.

Hot cocoa waits with marshmallow fluff,
As frosty air gets cold and tough.
Wrap up tight, don't catch a chill,
This frosted dream gives quite a thrill!

Laughter rings through frozen trees,
A winter dance with chilly breeze.
Look out, here comes the flying sled,
Who knew the cold could be so rad?

Icicle Serenade

Hanging sharp like nature's swords,
On rooftops high, they play some chords.
A tinkle here, a jingle there,
Icicles sway without a care.

Snowflakes tumble, twirl and glide,
Land on noses, won't abide.
A frozen face turns into glee,
As laughter spills from you and me.

A snowball fight, an epic scene,
The coldest battles ever seen!
Hearts so warm as fingers freeze,
In this icy world, we all must tease.

From rooftops high they start to drip,
With every thaw, we take a trip.
Winter's grip is holding tight,
But in our hearts, there's pure delight.

Shiver of Silence

The world is hushed, a blanket deep,
In frosty stillness, secrets creep.
Shivers dance upon the ground,
As silence reigns, a funny sound.

Through puffy coats and muffled yells,
Laughter rings, oh how it swells!
Around we twirl, a joyful sight,
Chasing each other, what a fright!

Cold noses press against the glass,
As we all wait for spring to pass.
A frosty breath, a steaming mug,
This chilly place, a winter hug.

With every crunch beneath our feet,
We share our cheer, nothing can beat.
A laugh echoes through this frost,
In winter's chill, we find our cost.

Frigid Fantasies

The air bites back, a zany tease,
We wear our scarves like silly ease.
A frosty breath, a giggle shared,
As mitten hands, together, paired.

Snowflakes tickle and whirl around,
Each one's wonder in silence found.
Children's laughter fills the space,
In winter's cold, we find our grace.

A slippery slope, a tumble, a roll,
All in good fun, that's how we stroll.
Each frosty breath brings hearty fun,
As winter days turn into one.

Hot soup awaits, the fire is bright,
'Tis a cozy scene on this frigid night.
In laughter's warmth, we'll always stay,
Chasing cold's bold games away!

The Shivery Joke

A penguin slipped on icy ground,
He made a sound, a funny sound.
He looked around, quite out of place,
With snowflakes dancing on his face.

A snowman tried to wear a hat,
But it fell down, oh what of that?
He laughed so loud, his nose did pop,
As snowballs flew, they made him stop.

A squirrel skated, lost his grip,
He did a twist, then made a flip.
He landed hard, a snowy mess,
And grinned instead of sheer distress.

With winter's chill, the jokes unfold,
Each frosty giggle never old.
In frozen air, the laughter grows,
As icy breezes tickle noses.

Chilling Revelations

A rabbit hopped in fuzzy fluff,
He turned around, said, "That's enough!"
With every leap, the snow would fly,
And soon he laughed, 'I can touch the sky!'

A polar bear in winter wear,
Lost his scarf while walking there.
He chased it fast, with comical grace,
Only to trip and smash his face.

A flock of geese in frozen flight,
Wore penguin suits, quite a sight!
They honked and squawked, so full of glee,
As winter winds blew raucously.

In chilling air, they frolic free,
These winter jesters, full of glee.
With every laugh, the cold retreats,
In frosty moments, joy repeats.

Frozen Parodies

A snowflake said, "I'm quite unique!"
But fell down fast, oh what a streak!
It landed soft on a puppy's nose,
And turned to giggles, as laughter grows.

A winter wind began to sing,
Of frosty times and foolish things.
It blew so strong, the branches swayed,
And tickled trees, this game they played.

A cold potato in a coat,
Tried to roll, but forgot to float.
It tumbled over, what a blunder,
And split apart like bolt from thunder!

In frozen realms where jesters play,
The chilly puns make winter sway.
A world of fun, where giggles rise,
Amidst the flakes that kiss the skies.

Whispers in the Wind

A snowy owl, with wise old eyes,
Told tales of laughter beneath the skies.
He winked and hooted, sharing delight,
As winter's chill danced all through the night.

A frosty breeze, with a mischievous grin,
Carried each joke, a playful spin.
With every gust, the humor flew,
Filling the air, like morning dew.

The icicles hung like teeth, so bright,
Their shimmer laughed in morning light.
And children played, in puffs of white,
Their giggles ringing, a pure delight.

In whispering winds, the laughter blends,
These chilly nights, where fun transcends.
Each frosty breath, a joyful sound,
In winter's grip, where joy is found.

Icebound Tales

A polar bear slipped on ice,
He didn't heed the weather's advice.
With a wiggle and a tumble,
He left us all to chuckle.

The penguins wore their best attire,
Sliding down on a winter tire.
With flippers flailing all around,
They formed a human snowman mound.

A snowman lost his carrot nose,
In a blizzard's fierce repose.
He looked around with frosty pride,
Then sneezed and watched his hat slide.

The chilly winds began to howl,
As yetis danced with a scowling owl.
We laughed so hard through frozen tears,
With ice-cold giggles, we conquered fears.

Permafrost Playwright

On stage, a walrus claimed the role,
With a pipe and top hat, so droll.
He tripped over his own flipper,
Creating laughs, the crowd grew snippier.

An arctic fox played a wise sage,
Spouting wisdom from a frosty page.
But each line was mixed with delight,
As he sneezed and vanished from sight.

A snowshoe hare in a tutu spun,
He danced around, a bundle of fun.
With each leap, he slipped and fell,
But brought down the house, oh what a sell!

Chillin' jesters filled the scene,
With ice cream cones and slushie machines.
They juggled snowballs, oh so grand,
A frosty spectacle, unplanned.

Hilarity in the Haze

In winter's mist, a moose did prance,
He twirled and stomped, lost in a dance.
His antlers caught a snowflake's kiss,
We laughed so hard, we couldn't miss.

A seal on skates began to glide,
With laughter ringing far and wide.
He spun around like a whirlwind, see,
And crashed right down—oh what glee!

The puffy clouds held secrets tight,
As polar bears wrestled with delight.
They rolled and tumbled, a frosty fight,
Creating joy in the cold, dark night.

With scarf and mittens, we joined the game,
Laughing so hard, no one felt shame.
In the frosty haze, we lost our cares,
Fun took flight in the snowy airs!

Polar Puns

Why do frostbite jokes make us laugh?
They're simply too cool, you can't do the math!
When a snowman tells a joke with flair,
He's always looking for a 'flurry' to share.

What did the ice cubes say to the sun?
We chill out here while you have your fun!
A snowflake kissed a penguin's nose,
And they giggled, "We're just here for the shows!"

Why don't pastels like snow? Too bright!
They prefer the gray—less glare, more light!
In this winter wonderland, jokes come alive,
Like ice sculptures that simply won't thrive!

As we toast with mugs of hot delight,
We chuckle warmly; no frostbite in sight.
The puns, like snowflakes, fall just right,
Creating laughter on this chilly night!

Crystal Ballad

Icicles hang like fairy lights,
The penguin's party's in full flight.
Hot cocoa drips from mugs so wide,
While everyone's bundled up inside.

Laughter echoes through the air,
A snowman tries to comb his hair.
Each snowflake falls with gentle grace,
But one gets stuck right on my face!

Sledding down the frozen hill,
I scream a little, but what a thrill.
With every bump, giggles erupt,
As I land with a snowy thump!

The cat just stares, her eyes so round,
At all the fluff that's on the ground.
She leaps and slips, oh what a sight,
As laughter fills the starry night.

Numbed Nonsense

Bundled up like a giant bear,
I shuffle clumsily through the air.
With earmuffs thick and gloves too tight,
I waddle weirdly left and right.

A snowball flies, my aim is poor,
It hits the neighbor at the door!
He shakes his fist, but I just grin,
A perfect way to start a win!

Hot soup awaits, oh what a treat,
Yet my frosty toes feel frozen feet.
As friends come in, they're looking pale,
Had they forgotten we'd need bail?

Outside the world looks crystal clear,
But inside's buzzing with joy and cheer.
With teacups clinking, giggles abound,
In this winter fun, joy is found.

Frosty Footprints

Tiny prints on the frosty lane,
Like little ghosts that dance again.
Materializing everywhere,
With every step, we leave a scare!

I make a snow angel, wings so wide,
The dog thinks I'm some weird slide.
With a bark and a leap he bounds,
While I'm face-first in chilly mounds!

We build a castle, tall and proud,
With turrets high, we'll scream aloud!
But then it wobbles, employees flee,
As we collapse in giggly glee.

With frosty noses, we march ahead,
A snowball fight, I'm filled with dread.
But it's all in fun, no frown in sight,
Let's revel in this snowy delight!

The Quiet Chill

In the moonlight, all looks bright,
But chilly whispers steal the night.
With frozen toes, I hop and shout,
As frostbite starts to creep about.

We plan a race, but slip and slide,
One leap forward, two steps aside.
The laughter rings, it's quite absurd,
As we freeze while dodging the bird!

The cat just stares, wide eyes like plates,
Watching us dance 'round the snowdrifts' gates.
A snowball flies, it sails right by,
And drips of laughter float to the sky!

Yet still we love this winter spree,
With icicles as our jewelry.
In the quiet chill, full of fun,
We embrace the cold 'til day is done.

Icy Antics of the Season

A penguin slipped on frozen ice,
With a wobble that was quite precise.
He danced around, legs akimbo,
Yelling, 'Look at me! I'm a limbo!'

A snowman sneezed, his nose was stuck,
He shivered too, that poor old muck.
With a frosty grin and a chilly wiggle,
He yelled, 'Someone pass me a warm snuggle!'

The rabbits hop in fluffy boots,
Preparing for their winter hoots.
They slide and glide, what a sight,
With cotton tails that shimmer so bright!

The kids in layers, all thick and round,
Tumble down the hills with a joyful sound.
They giggle and squeal, it's just a blast,
Rolling and bouncing, they'll stick and slide fast!

Laughing Through the Frost

A frosty breeze blew through the trees,
Carrying laughter, swirling with ease.
A squirrel slipped with a nut in tow,
And giggled as it rolled in a frosty glow.

The icicles hung with laughable finesse,
Like comedians dressed in winter's best dress.
With every drip, they crack jokes anew,
'We might melt, but we'll freeze with the view!'

Children build forts like grand castles fair,
And argue about who's the king of the air.
'With snowballs as ammo, I'm top-notch tonight!'
They battle with giggles, what a silly sight!

As evening falls, stars begin to peek,
They shimmer and twinkle; the sky's at its peak.
The frost draws near with its chilly embrace,
While raucous laughter warms up the place!

Chilly Chuckles Beneath the Stars

Beneath the moon, a snowball flies,
Aimed at Frank, who yelps and cries.
Yet laughter bubbles, rises in cheer,
As winter's chill becomes their dear.

Hot cocoa spills from a carton, oh dear!
The dog in the winter jumps in with cheer.
A whirl of fur, chocolate, and snow,
He shakes it off, with a playful show.

The owls perched high gave a hoot and a wink,
Witnessing clowns with frosty pink.
They rocked on limbs, in the cold night's sight,
Their giggles echoing, oh what delight!

The stars are twinkling, a blanket of laughs,
As laughter softens the icy drafts.
Under this sky, friendships are made,
Through chilly chuckles, winter won't fade!

Humor in the Heart of Winter

A snowflake danced, it fancied its grace,
But landed on a dog's snooty face.
With a shake and a sneeze, it took to the sky,
'I'm the flake that tickled your high and dry!'

Old man Jenkins built a tall tower,
But his hat blew off like a winter flower.
Chasing it down with a laugh and a shout,
He slipped on his wand, sending it all about!

The cats in scarves, strutting with pride,
Thought they were queens on a frosty ride.
With tails held high, and a pompous strut,
They laughed at the dogs who couldn't keep up!

At the end of the day, as the sun takes a seat,
Winter reminds us, with a giggle and beat.
For in every flake and each icy breeze,
Lies humor that warms like a cozy tease!

Ice Laughs

The frosty breeze does tickle the nose,
While icicles hang like frozen prose.
Unicorns in slippers slide on the ground,
They giggle and wiggle, a sight to be found.

Chattering teeth compose a choir,
As bundled snowmen dance by the fire.
They throw snowballs with glee in their eyes,
Their laughter erupts, as the winter flies.

Pine trees donned in white fluffy hats,
Invite a penguin to sit and chat.
With jokes on their lips, they tumble about,
While winter's chill brings all of these shouts.

So let's embrace this chilly delight,
Where tongues can freeze but smiles are bright.
We'll roast marshmallows, hear stories unfold,
In a world where the air sparkles bold.

Jests under the Ice

Beneath the frost, the humor hides,
With penguins in bow ties, strutting like guides.
They waddle and flap, looking quite prim,
As icy breezes make their cheeks dim.

A polar bear plays chess with a seal,
Checkmate! They yell, what a big deal!
A walrus gives high-fives with his tusks,
Yet giggles escape, in frosty gusts.

Snowflakes like confetti drift from above,
Their landing, a soft kiss, a chilly hug.
A snowman lost his hat in the gale,
But wore a potato, the funniest tale!

Hats fly away, but spirits stay near,
Chatter and chuckles warm up the cheer.
In winter's embrace, we find such delight,
Where laughter shines bright throughout the night.

Frozen Frivolity

In the land of frost, where the wild things play,
Ice skaters twirl, come join in the fray.
With banana peels tossed on the rink,
Slips and laughter, faster than you think!

The winter sun shines with mischief and glee,
Irritated squirrels throw acorns with spree.
Their furry, vexed faces cracking a grin,
As snowflakes fall down, a flurry begins.

A snowball fight breaks like an avalanche,
Hilarity strikes, oh, take a chance!
With each toss, a giggle, a gentle poke,
Jack Frost himself cannot help but choke!

In the chill of the night, we gather around,
Hot cocoa and jokes, our joy knows no bound.
Let's freeze time in laughter, our hearts won't race,
In this land of frivolity, find your place.

Mirth in the Mist

Through snowy canyons and icy trees,
Comes a jolly elf dancing with ease.
He slips on a patch, then tumbles right down,
Making snow angels while wearing a frown!

A clever rabbit hops in a parade,
Wearing a scarf he expertly made.
He jests with the wolves, who howl for more,
As the mist envelops this playful lore.

The moonlight glimmers on frosted peaks,
As friends share stories and laughter peaks.
Each freezing word wraps us up tight,
While snowflakes twirl, dancing with delight.

So gather your mittens, bring forth the fun,
In this laughter-filled land where we run.
With a wink and a nod, we'll conquer the chill,
In a world where joy and jest never will.

Witty Winter Whims

The penguins wear their little ties,
They dance around as the snowflakes fly.
Snowmen dream of beachy fun,
While chilly breezes make everyone run.

Hot cocoa spills, a marshmallow fight,
Giggling children, what a sight!
Sleds slide down, a wild race,
All bundled up, with smiles on each face.

Icicles dangle like pointy teeth,
The fairy lights twinkle beneath.
Frosty breath escapes in a puff,
Winter's games can be quite tough!

But laughter echoes through the air,
As mittened hands try to throw snow with flair.
In this chill, a warmth we find,
With quirky moments that are one of a kind!

Humor amid the Icicles

The rooftops sport their icy crowns,
While snowflakes fall like little clowns.
The dogs prance in their fluffy gear,
Chasing snowflakes, never fear!

Frosty windows, a nice surprise,
Witty doodles in frozen guise.
While grandma's knitting gets tangled tight,
She laughs aloud, what a silly sight!

Glistening paths where slips abound,
With every fall, there's laughter found.
Sliding down a hill with a whoop,
The cold air's filled with giggly troop.

Hot pies cooling on the sill,
As winter plays with a sneaky thrill.
Yet jokes are shared as a frosty wind blows,
In this chilly dance, joy overflows!

Frost Enchantment

The crystal flakes like tiny stars,
Filling silence, near and far.
A friendly snowball whizzes by,
Hitting someone, oh my, oh my!

Sledding down the hilly ride,
With squeals of joy we cannot hide.
A snow globe dance, we twirl around,
In this brisk wonder, laughter's found.

The frozen pond, a gleaming sight,
With twirling skaters, pure delight.
And when the frosty wind gives a blow,
It tickles noses, making us glow.

Wooly hats and scarves galore,
As we shiver, who could ask for more?
These moments freeze, yet warm our hearts,
In winter's grip, the fun never departs!

Under the Winter Moon

The moon hangs high on a silver thread,
While cozy blankets warm our bed.
A cat in a sweater, looking chic,
As we laugh until we can barely speak.

With snowflakes twirling in the night,
Creating chaos that feels just right.
We build a fort, a fortress grand,
With mismatched toys and a snowman band.

The chilly night air whispers sweet,
As friends come over, laughter's treat.
Hot pies burning, oh what a fuss,
We leave the kitchen and take a bus!

While outside, snowflakes swirl and play,
With a giggle here and a snowball's sway.
Beneath this moon, laughter's the tune,
In frosty fun, we're all marooned!

Quietly Cryogenic

The frosty air bites like a prank,
Icicles dangle, a chilly tank.
Sipping hot cocoa, we shiver and shake,
With every sip, a frozen wake.

Laughter erupts with each brisk breeze,
Feet in the snow, like clumsy bees.
We trip on ice, oh, what a scene,
Winter's slapstick, hilariously keen.

Bundled up tight, we waddle and roam,
In layers of wool, we look far from home.
A snowball fight breaks out in the park,
The laughter ignites, a delightful spark.

Silent snow falls as we play our part,
Creating a canvas for every heart.
With each friendly throw and each playful shove,
We find in the cold what we truly love.

Humor in the Frost

Under gray skies, we gather in cheer,
Laughter abounds as the frost draws near.
A snowman stands with a crooked grin,
A carrot nose, it's all for the win.

Jokesters slip on paths of ice,
With every fall, we chuckle twice.
Winter woes wrapped in scarves so bright,
Let's stand together, it's pure delight.

Hot cider warms our chilled-out souls,
As laughter echoes, the warmth console.
Snowflakes dance, they twirl like fools,
In winter's chill, we redefine rules.

With frosty breaths that resemble clouds,
We dance in freeze, amidst nature's shrouds.
Facing the cold with a smile so wide,
In this chilly world, our joy can't hide.

Tundra Tidbits

Oh, the winter, a frosty delight,
We bundle so tight, like mummies in flight.
With snow on our noses and laughter in tow,
The magic of winter lends itself to glow.

Hats bobbing high, we parade around,
With sleds and toboggans, laughter resounds.
Falling like snowflakes, we slip and slide,
In the comedy of winter, let joy reside.

A snowball fight erupts, like a crazy war,
Hurling soft fluff, we can't help but roar.
The cold can't contain the glee we create,
While winter's embraced, we celebrate fate.

We dig in the snow, like kids on a quest,
Building our kingdoms, we give it our best.
In the chill we find warmth, in the ice we laugh,
Tundra's giving us humor, our heartfelt craft.

The Jests of Winter

In jackets so poofy, we waddle around,
Chasing the snowflakes that fall to the ground.
With cheeks painted red, we tumble and scoff,
Winter's wild game, we just can't get off.

Sledding down hills, a swift comedic glide,
Flying through powder, pure joy as our guide.
With each twist and tumble, we giggle and shout,
The frosty season, a playful layout.

Hot chocolate spills, oops! What a scene,
Giggles erupt, we're the winter's routine.
With mittens so chunky, we toss and we play,
In this frozen world, we dance the day away.

At night we gather, sharing tales of our day,
Of slipping on ice and the wild fun at play.
In the heart of winter, we find the best measure,
A bounty of laughter, our greatest treasure.

The Silently Shivering Game

In the winter's frosty grip,
We play a game of who can slip.
With noses red and laughter loud,
We tumble softly in the crowd.

Hot cocoa and funny hats,
All bundled up like furry rats.
We dance around the icy trees,
And try to dodge the biting breeze.

When the chill begins to bite,
We giggle and pretend to fight.
Sliding down the slopes with ease,
Squealing like a bunch of bees.

In this freezing, laughing mess,
We wear our jackets, they're a dress!
With each shiver, joy we claim,
In winter's world, it's all a game.

Frozen Shenanigans

The snowflakes fall, a comic scene,
As penguins plot, what could it mean?
With snowmen dancing, oh what a sight,
Their carrot noses twist in delight.

Ice skating on a pond that's slick,
I'm not a swan, but I can kick!
With flailing arms and wiggles so wide,
I spin and fall, my hopes deride.

Hot chocolate spills, I start to scream,
My marshmallow mountain, an epic dream!
With giggles and grins, we roam the white,
In the field of frosty, pure delight.

Our frozen friends, they wave and cheer,
Embracing winter, year after year.
Through icy winds and shivers galore,
We find the joy in winter's roar.

Witty Winds of Winter

The wind is teasing, oh, what a breeze,
It lifts our hats with playful ease.
We chase them down the snowy lane,
Laughter echoes, driving us insane.

My gloves have vanished, oh where'd they go?
The joke's on me; it's quite the show!
With frozen fingers and rosy cheeks,
We frolic on, no time for weeks.

A snowball fight is on the cue,
I'm a stubborn target, that much is true.
When will I learn this lesson cold?
That winter fun never gets old.

The winds are witty, full of cheer,
They spin us 'round, then disappear.
In every gust, there's joy to find,
Winter's punchline, oh so kind!

The Jester's Frozen Breath

A jester laughs with frozen breath,
Cracking jokes like winter's theft.
With chilly air, he spins his tale,
Of frosty fumbles in the pale.

His hat is tall, it flops just right,
He juggles snowballs, what a sight!
We cheer him on with clapping hands,
As laughter bubbles in icy strands.

In every joke, a snowflake's dance,
He makes us giggle, gives us a chance.
To find the joy in icy air,
And wear our silliness like a flair.

With frozen fingers and grinning glee,
The jester knows the best decree:
That winter's chill can bring us near,
Through laughs and warmth, we hold so dear.

Radiant Frost

When winter's breath wraps tight like a hug,
We slip and slide on icy rugs.
Hot cocoa calls, it's time to cheer,
As snowflakes dance, it's laugh-out-loud here.

With mittens thick and hats askew,
We build a snowman, like a clown, not blue.
But all that snow, a fluffy trap,
I lost my shoe in a snowy flap!

The chill creeps in, yet we don't mind,
We snicker at frost, oh so unkind.
The wind gives a swish, a playful tease,
While icicles dangle from branches, with ease.

So let the blizzards come and play,
We'll wear our socks in a colorful array.
For laughter echoes through this frost,
In winter's grip, we'll never be lost.

Echoes of the Icy Realm

In the realm where icicles cling,
A frozen symphony, we take wing.
With cheeks like cherries, laughter loud,
We're jolly jesters, winter's crowd.

A snowball flies, aimed just right,
But I duck down for a playful fright.
Frigid air bites, a playful jab,
As we slip and tumble, a comic grab!

With sleds that zoom and laughter's fit,
Life's little mishaps, we can't quit.
Every frost and flake, a giggle waits,
As we race against the chilly fates.

So stir the cocoa, let's huddle near,
For in this winter, there's much to cheer.
With echoes of laughter in icy climes,
We'll boast of our adventures and funny times!

The Twinkle of Chill

The chill in the air whispers, 'Let's play!'
With a twinkle of ice, we're here to stay.
Boots stomp loud on a crackling floor,
As flurries tumble with a frosty roar.

A snowman beckons, we give it a hat,
But up it flies, oh dear, how 'bout that?
With rosy cheeks, we bounce and slip,
In this winter circus, we tumble and trip.

Hot chocolate spills, a sweet delight,
We wear it proudly, what a sight!
Marshmallow snowflakes, they float and land,
In our frozen kingdom, it's perfectly planned.

So let's embrace this frosty flaunt,
With giggles galore, in our winter haunt.
For every icy tingle, there's joy to behold,
In this wonderland where the stories are bold.

Frosted Whimsy

In the frosted air, we twirl around,
With laughter and giggles, the best kind of sound.
Slipping and sliding, we hit the ground,
In this whimsical winter, joy is abound.

The snowflakes whisper as they fall,
Each one a jester, some funny, some small.
We chase the sleds down a slickened spree,
With warmth in our hearts, how silly we be!

Frost-covered cheeks, noses all red,
As we plan our heist for warm bread spread.
With snow in our boots, giggling all the way,
We'll craft our own magic, come what may!

So gather 'round snug with candies in hand,
In this frosted kingdom, we're a merry band.
With whimsy and laughs, let the chill reign high,
In this playful winter, we'll soar and fly!

Giggles from the Glacial Depths

In the depths where frost does play,
The snowmen dance, hip-hip-hooray!
With carrot noses set just right,
They break into a wobbly flight.

Fluffy flakes start to tickle toes,
As ice cubes laugh with how it goes.
A penguin slips, a comedy show,
With every tumble, giggles flow.

Snowball fights turn into a game,
With all the friends shouting their names.
But watch your back, a cheeky throw,
Can turn a fling into a snow show.

So gather round, let joy abound,
In the winter's fun, we're tightly bound.
For laughter sprouts where cold winds blow,
In this frosty land, the smiles grow.

Laughter in the Luminous Snow

Under blankets of twinkling white,
Cheeky snowflakes dance in the light.
A jolly snowman cracks a joke,
While polar bears wear hats bespoke.

Sleds zip past with happy cheers,
As frosty air brings silly sneers.
A flurry of snowballs in the air,
With each one tossed, we've not a care.

Snow angels stretch with arms so wide,
As giggles echo, we can't hide!
The coldest winds bring the loudest laughs,
And warm our hearts in frigid drafts.

So bundle up in bright, warm layers,
With twinkling eyes and silly flares.
For in this world of gleaming snow,
Each laugh is bright, our spirits glow.

Whispers of the Winter Wits

The trees wear coats of sparkling white,
While all around shines pure delight.
Snowflakes giggle, swirling round,
In this winter trap, joy is found.

A snowball hit—a loud surprise!
With frozen chuckles, laughter flies.
Mittens tossed and scarves gone rogue,
In the winter's fun, we're all a brogue.

A chilly breeze shares witty tales,
Of snowshoeing dogs with furry trails.
Each little joke floats on the air,
As frozen hearts shed every care.

So brew some cocoa, add some cheer,
For winter's humor is drawing near.
With every chuckle, spirits lift,
In the icy air, our hearts swift.

The Sly Side of Chill

The wind plays tricks, with icy glee,
While snowflakes whisper, 'Can you see?'
A rabbit hops in boots of red,
With frozen feet, laughs fill our heads.

Icicles dangle like frozen teeth,
A winter's smile, a true mischief.
With every slip, there's joy to share,
As we tumble down without a care.

Hot cocoa pots seem to chuckle too,
As warmth invites our laughter through.
Frosty puns on the tips of tongues,
In this chilly world, we're forever young.

So gather friends, embrace the frost,
For in this cold, we're never lost.
With every joke that takes a flight,
We find the fun in frosty nights.

Jesting with Jack Frost

Jack Frost came to play, oh what a sight,
With icy fingers, he'd give you a fright.
He tickles noses, makes cheeks so red,
While sneaking up to chill the warmest bed.

His laughter echoes through the frozen trees,
As he whispers jokes carried by the breeze.
We slip and slide, fall into the fluff,
Yet every tumble just adds to the stuff.

Snowballs fly with a mischievous aim,
Making winter wonderland a silly game.
With every slip, we share a loud cheer,
As Jack keeps laughing, he's always near!

In the midst of white, we dance with glee,
For winter's humor is plain to see.
So let's embrace this frosty delight,
With Jack's jests bringing warmth to the night.

Cold Conundrums and Warm Smiles

When winter comes, we bundle tight,
Yet laughter spills into the night.
Cold fingers fumble, hats fly away,
Creating chaos in a frosty ballet.

Hot cocoa spills, oh what a mess,
Marshmallows float in winter's dress.
With rosy cheeks, we laugh so loud,
As snowflakes dance like a giggling crowd.

Ice skating turns into a wobbly race,
Each slip and slide adds humor to the space.
"Watch out!" we shout as we lose control,
With every fall, we regain our soul.

So let's toast to the chill with a grin,
For these frosty times make warmth within.
Each conundrum wrapped in a chill embrace,
Turns shivers to giggles in this merry place.

A Frosty Tale of Merriment

In a land so white where the snowflakes twirl,
Lived a funny fellow with a frosty swirl.
He threw the cold like a playful jest,
Turning winter's grasp into a frosty fest.

With every flake that fell from the sky,
He conjured up laughter, oh me, oh my!
A snowman chuckles, a snowdog prances,
In this chilly realm, everyone dances.

Frosty battles with snowball might,
Turn serious moments into sheer delight.
"Oh dear!" we cry in a flurry of glee,
As snowflakes tumble and dance carefree.

So we gather 'round in this frosted tale,
With laughter ringing like a joyful gale.
For in the freeze, we find our warm light,
In a frosty tale that lasts through the night.

Frostbitten Fables

Once in a town, the frost came bright,
Turning day into a sparkly night.
Where mittens vanished, and scarves took flight,
In a hilarious battle with Jack's frosty bite.

A creature emerged with a mischievous grin,
Wrapped in snow, oh, where to begin?
Teasing the kids to catch him with ease,
"My legs are frozen! Oh, help me please!"

As they chased him 'round in this frozen fun,
Tripping over snowdrifts, each slip was a pun.
Gales of laughter followed their plight,
In the frosty air, every stumble felt right.

So when winter calls with its frosty fables,
Let's join the fun, gather our tables.
For in every chill, and every twist,
Live stories of frolic that simply can't be missed.

Jolly in the Frozen Kingdom

In the kingdom of frost, where the cold winds blow,
Laughter rings out, letting good cheer flow.
Snowmen get frosty in their top hat attire,
While penguins in tuxedos dance with desire.

Chilly air tickles, making noses turn red,
While kids with snowballs pelt a brave sled.
Hot cocoa awaits by the crackling fire,
As winter's wild humor takes us higher.

Gliding on ice, a slip and a slide,
In this chilly delight, we all take pride.
With each little tumble, a giggle erupts,
In this frigid kingdom, winter's joy is abrupt.

So let's bundle up and embrace this cheer,
With frosty follies bringing us near.
For in this wonderland, full of jolly glee,
The cold makes us laugh, oh can't you see?

Frosty Tales of Merry Mischief

Once upon a time in a wintery delight,
Mischief was brewing under the moonlight.
A snowball brigade took to the streets,
With snowmen as targets, oh, what a feat!

A squirrel in mittens flew past the trees,
Chasing his acorn in the brisk breeze.
He slipped and he slid on an ice slicked path,
We laughed as he fumbled in a wintery bath.

Elves with hot chocolate, all merrily churn,
Snuck in the back while the cocoa would burn.
As the marshmallows danced in the pot with glee,
We feasted and chuckled, oh what a spree!

So gather around for tales so bright,
In a world of frosty, hilarious sight.
With giggles and grins, we warmly recall,
The frosty mischief that conquered us all.

Winter Whiskeys and Witty Words.

Gather 'round the hearth with glasses in hand,
Where laughter and stories meet winter's demand.
With sips of warm whiskey and quips on our lips,
We toast to the season, let merriment rip!

A wink from the snowflakes that swirl in the air,
Brings warmth to our hearts, feeling light without care.
Each tale gets taller with each warming sip,
As we giggle and snicker, let laughter just rip.

Frosty the drinker, with his beard of snow,
Tries to tell jokes, but they're icy and slow.
Yet still, we chuckle, with tears in our eyes,
As winter's warm whiskey keeps us in high ties.

So let's raise a glass to this chilly retreat,
With witty words spoken, humor so sweet.
In the heart of the winter, we find pure delight,
With warmth in our bellies and laughter so bright!

Winter's Whisper

Whispers of winter float softly and sly,
As chilly winds chuckle, oh my, oh my!
The trees wear their blankets of fluffy white coats,
Each branch a perch for the wind's witty jotes.

A rabbit in boots hops with funky flair,
Trying so hard to avoid the cold air.
The frost plays tricks, like a mischief-filled sprite,
Turning swings into sleds under the pale moonlight.

Fireside tales spin with giggles and glee,
Of creatures in scarves having snowball jubilee.
With every crisp crunch, it's a laugh we ignite,
In the magic of winter, where humor takes flight.

So gather your friends, let the fun ideas bloom,
In winter's cool calm, we banish all gloom.
For in each frosty moment, laughter will spread,
As winter's soft whispers light up our head.

Icy Intrigue

The penguins waddle, oh so bold,
In jackets tight, they're feeling cold.
A snowball fight, what a delight,
But someone slipped and took a flight!

Frosty breath dances in the air,
While friends pretend they just don't care.
They drink hot chocolate by the fires,
Laughing at each other's mishires!

A squirrel dons a tiny hat,
Digging through the snow – how's that?
He finds a stash of frozen fries,
And munches happily with sighs!

When icicles start to form and drip,
Watch out for splashes, take a trip!
It's slips and slides all through the day,
In winter's hooks, we laugh and play!

Winter's Chuckle

Oh, what's that? A snowman stood,
With carrots lost, not looking good.
He's been to parties, made some rounds,
With whiskey-flavored melted sounds!

Snowflakes play on noses bright,
As kids throw snowballs, what a sight!
A dog runs past, slips on his tail,
Face-first in snow, with a loud wail!

The trees wear blankets, all so white,
As laughter echoes through the night.
The winter air is sharp and clear,
As friends share jokes, and holiday cheer!

Frosted windows tell our tale,
Of frozen giggles in the gale.
A chorus of joy, in the crisp cold,
We bundle up, young and old!

Glittering Gags

With chilly toes, we stomp and dance,
In icy boots, we take a chance.
Wit is sharp as winter's bite,
We spin and twirl with all our might!

A snow globe magic, we watch and stare,
As snowflakes swirl without a care.
A candy cane toss, oops—there it goes,
Right into the snowman's nose!

The frozen pond, a proper stage,
For little skaters, full of rage.
One goes down, the crowd erupts,
With giggles loud and flailing limbs!

So grab your gloves and join the fun,
Chasing shadows 'til the day is done.
In winter's grip, we find delight,
With funny moments, chilly nights!

Chilly Revelries

The frost is gleaming, oh what a game,
With laughter echoing, just the same.
A blizzard twirls, the kids complain,
But joy remains in snowflakes' reign!

A cat in boots, so proud and sly,
Chasing after shadows drifting by.
Heads turn quickly toward the sight,
As everyone roars with pure delight!

Icicle teeth, a jagged grin,
Where laughter starts, let joy begin.
Through winter wonder, we frolic fast,
Creating memories that forever last!

In the crisp air, our spirits soar,
As bundled up, we beg for more.
With frosty fingers and cheeks so red,
We cherish moments, fun instead!

Frigid Farce Beneath the Moon

Under the moon, the wind does dance,
Frosty friends in a silly prance.
They slip and slide, a comical show,
Wearing big boots, but moving slow.

The snowman frowns, his carrot's awry,
His arms are sticks, he looks a bit shy.
A snowball flies, just missed my head,
I laugh so hard, I tumble instead.

Icicles hang like teeth out of place,
Every breath steams up the wintry space.
The laughter echoes through the night,
Making the chill feel oh so light.

In the frosty air, our voices cheer,
Winter's punchline is finally here!
With playful hearts and smiles aglow,
The frigid farce puts on a show!

Glacial Giggles and Frosty Frivolities

With slushy boots, we march outside,
Ice patches lurking, we cannot hide.
Each step is laughter, each slip a cheer,
Making memories we hold so dear.

The kids build castles, winter's delight,
While I throw snowballs, with all my might.
Joy fills the air, the snowflakes dance,
In this glacial giggle, we take our chance.

A snow dog barks with a frosty grin,
Chasing the flakes as they swirl and spin.
His ears flap wildly in the brisk breeze,
He trips on a pile, oh what a tease!

Curl up with cocoa, a marshmallow tower,
Winter's comedy in every hour.
With glistening frost and grins so wide,
We revel in joys that starkly slide!

Comedic Chills of the Season

Frosty noses and squinty eyes,
We brave the chill under winter skies.
The neighbors' lights twinkle with glee,
While snowflakes tickle just like a bee.

A squirrel dressed warmly looks quite absurd,
He steals my hat, oh, the nerve of that bird!
I chase him down, don't trip on a patch,
But he scampers off, oh what a catch!

The puppy digs deep, what fun he makes,
Stirring up frost and tumbling flakes.
With wagging tails and goofy spins,
We laugh out loud, winter's silly wins.

Hot chocolate spills, a playful mess,
With each little slip, our spirits press.
Through comedic chills, we take delight,
In the season's mirth, all day and night!

The Playful Ice Capade

On this wintry stage, we twirl and glide,
With frosty hats and hearts open wide.
The ice capade glimmers, a frolicking sight,
Where laughter and warmth make spirits bright.

We dance on the ice, but some take a tumble,
As giggles erupt and woes turn to humble.
A twist and a spin, who's the next to fall?
In this playful chaos, we're all having a ball!

Snowflakes are falling, a heavenly play,
Building our castles until the day.
A snowball fight breaks out with a shout,
In such joyous antics, we dance about.

Together we cheer, no need for a crown,
In our winter kingdom, we won't wear a frown.
With hot cider ready, let the laughter invade,
Enjoying the thrill of the ice capade!

The Frosty Tease

The air bites back, a playful snare,
My nose turns red, like a ripe cherry,
Puffs of breath float like tiny ghosts,
As I dance with chill, feeling merry.

Icicles hang like pearly teeth,
The hat on my head is a daring feat,
I slip and slide, a graceful fool,
In this icy wonderland, life's a duel.

Snowflakes fall, a soft parade,
Laughter echoes, we're all dismayed,
A snowman grins with a carrot nose,
Yet I'm the punchline, nobody knows.

So bring on the shivers, let's laugh it out,
I'll wear my mittens, without a doubt,
With frozen fingers, we share our joys,
In this frosty tease, we're just silly boys.

Glimmering in the Cold

Under the stars, with frosty sight,
We waddle like penguins, what a sight!
Frosty eyebrows, like old grandpas,
Our laughter rings, despite the flaws.

Trees dressed in white, jewels aglow,
We build our forts, let the fun flow,
With snowball fights, and playful shouts,
In this chilled air, joy never doubts.

Slippers on ice, I take a slide,
Wishing for warmth, but I've got pride,
Each frozen step, a chance to grin,
With mittens lost, let the mischief begin!

The moonlight glimmers, a silent cheer,
As snowflakes twirl, we persevere,
In the cold embrace, we find delight,
Together we frolic through the starry night.

The Wintry Chronicles

Once upon a time, in a frosty land,
Where snowmen giggled, oh so grand,
We layered up, three coats thick,
Yet outside, our fingers would still play tricks.

Sleds zoom past, with reckless glee,
I tumble down, in a blaze of spree,
Hot cocoa waits, a warming balm,
But first, let's laugh, it's a winter's calm.

Frigid air gives us rosy cheeks,
In this frozen world, humor speaks,
Each frosty breath, a spectacle grand,
With each slide and stumble, it's all just planned.

Our wintry tales, a jolly cheer,
In bright snowy days, we hold them dear,
So gather 'round, for stories untold,
Of laughter and warmth, as we grow old.

Breezy Banter

The wind's a comedian, with jokes so sly,
Whipping my scarf as I stumble by,
Each gust of laughter lifts me anew,
As I chase my hat that just flew.

Frosty fingers, yet spirits soar,
With every chuckle, we ask for more,
We trip on ice and spin around,
In this fun-filled chaos, joy is found.

A blizzard's whisper plays pranks on we,
Snowflakes giggle, can't you see?
Breezy banter, we're all in jest,
Chillin' together, it's simply the best.

So wrap up tight, let the chill embrace,
As frosty humor puts smiles on our face,
Let's toast to winter, with laughter bold,
In the chill of the air, tales of warmth unfold.

The Sleepy Frost

Pajamas tucked, I shiver tight,
The window gleams, a frosty sight.
My breath, a cloud, it dances free,
I swear it whispers, 'Get hot tea!'

A sea of white, it's all around,
In every crunch, a muffled sound.
The world's a snooze, no one's awake,
Except my nose, it has a ache!

Slippers missing, oh what a plight,
I hop around, in sheer delight.
With chilly toes, I march and twirl,
Like penguin prance, I give a whirl!

The morning laughs, the sun peeks shy,
I toss on hats, oh me, oh my!
As icicles drip and breath has steam,
Who knew that cold could be such a dream?

Joy in the Freeze

With mittens on, I'm feeling fine,
I build a man with carrot wine.
He's got a smile, oh what a sight,
In this chill, we laugh outright!

A snowball fight, I take my aim,
The neighbor yells, 'Now that's a shame!'
But giggles burst, no one's annoyed,
In winters fun, we are overjoyed.

We slide on slopes, the thrill is real,
Our squeals of joy, a happy squeal!
With every tumble, laughter rolls,
What's winter's chill? It warms our souls!

The fluff is thick, the fun won't cease,
Hot cocoa waits, a sweet release.
In every freeze, we find our cheer,
Joy spreads wide, our hearts sincere!

Frigid Antics

My nose is red, my cheeks are pink,
I dive right in; let's see what's linked!
A snowman shouts, 'You knock like that?'
With frozen arms, he sounds quite flat!

A slip and slide, oh what a fall,
I tumble hard; I give my all.
The dog does dance, he prances near,
With frosty breath, we share a cheer!

Sleds go flying, oh what a blast,
Around we zip, winter's spell is cast.
With rosy cheeks, we scream and play,
Each frozen moment brings joy our way!

Laughter echoes, it fills the air,
In frosty days, there's fun to spare.
Who knew that cold could feel so warm?
In winter's grip, we thrive, we swarm!

The Cold Hard Truth

The forecast says, don't be misled,
With layers on, I waddle ahead.
The world may freeze, the wind may bite,
But here I stand, dressed up just right!

My coffee's cold, it taunts and teases,
While jackets bulk, my fashion freezes.
I laugh and sip, with all my might,
In this chilly place, I feel so bright!

Chill sends shivers, that is a fact,
But we just giggle and keep intact.
So gather round, share laughs galore,
The winter's cold brings us in store!

In frozen air, life's still a dance,
Each icy gust, we take a chance.
So here's a toast, 'neath icy skies,
For frosty fun, just watch us rise!